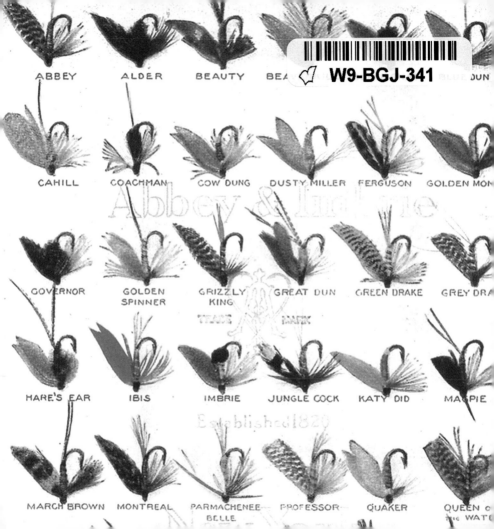

ABBEY   ALDER   BEAUTY   BEA...   BLUE DUN

CAHILL   COACHMAN   COW DUNG   DUSTY MILLER   FERGUSON   GOLDEN MON...

GOVERNOR   GOLDEN SPINNER   GRIZZLY KING   GREAT DUN   GREEN DRAKE   GREY DRA...

HARE'S EAR   IBIS   IMBRIE   JUNGLE COCK   KATY DID   MAGPIE

MARCH BROWN   MONTREAL   PARMACHENEE BELLE   PROFESSOR   QUAKER   QUEEN of THE WAT...

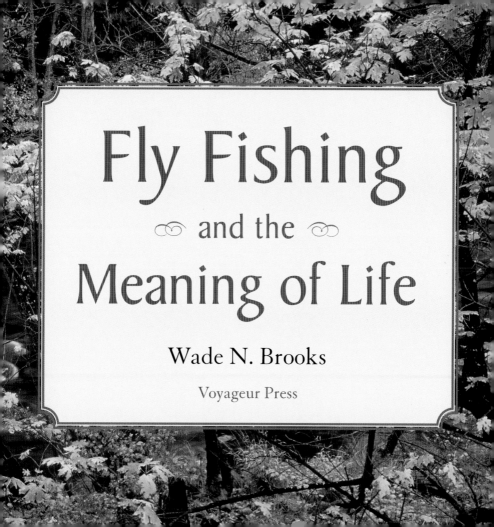

Fly Fishing

⌦ and the ⌫

Meaning of Life

Wade N. Brooks

Voyageur Press

First published in 2006 by Voyageur Press, an imprint of MBI Publishing Company, Galtier Plaza, Suite 200, 380 Jackson Street, St. Paul, MN 55101-3885 USA

MBI Publishing Company titles are also available at discounts in bulk quantity for industrial or sales-promotional use. For details write to Special Sales Manager at MBI Publishing Company, Galtier Plaza, Suite 200, 380 Jackson Street, St. Paul, MN 55101-3885 USA

Brooks, Wade N.
  Fly fishing and the meaning of life /
Wade N. Brooks.
    p. cm
  ISBN-13: 978-0-7603-2575-9
  ISBN-10: 0-7603-2575-8
  1. Fly fishing—Pictorial works. 2. Fly fishing—Quotations, maxims, etc. I Title.
  SH456.B723 2006
   799.12'40222—dc22

                              2006000012

Edited by Danielle J. Ibister
Designed by Maria Friedrich

Printed in China

On the front cover: *Vintage lithograph by James C. McKell*

On the spine: *Blue Damsel streamer fly*

On the endpapers: *1929 Abbey & Imbrie advertisement*

On the frontispiece: *Fly box*
(Photograph © R. Valentine Atkinson)

On the title page: *Angler on the Sacramento River*
(Photograph © R. Valentine Atkinson)

On the back cover: *Angler tying on fly*
(Photograph © R. Valentine Atkinson)

FISH BY BAROMETER—Know When They Will Bite

Field & Stream

LATEST
Fish Laws
Seasons, Limits and Licenses

June 1939
15¢

To the Reader

Since Sir Izaak Walton's time, fly fishing has been a sport of contemplation, of quietude, and—eventually—of wisdom. To cast a fly for trout in a remote stream is to ponder the meaning of life, love, religion, and dry flies.

But before an angler reaches a state of enlightenment, there are a few bumps along the stream. Learning to cast without breaking off every fly. Staying upright in waders. Tying on a Royal Coachman while standing in a rushing river. Spending hundreds— or thousands—on gear. Matching the hatch. Explaining to your spouse why you spend every weekend on the river. Mastering everything—and then accepting that you'll be releasing every fish you catch.

Fly fishing is one of the most challenging recreational pursuits an individual can undertake. It tests one's mind, body, and patience. This challenge has provoked a host of aphorisms, insights, and wisecracks about the sport—all presented for your pleasure in these pages.

This classic fly fisherman was painted by sporting artist Arthur Davenport Fuller (1889–1966), whose work graced many Field & Stream *covers over the years.*

> "A trout is a moment of beauty known only to those who seek it."
>
> ARNOLD GINGRICH

Bob White

Wildlife artist Bob White captures a moment of beauty in this original watercolor, One Last Look.

"Fly Fishers are notorious for not explaining what they are doing to their spouses or strangers. It is too complicated, they think, or else it is like jazz in Louis Armstrong's paradox: if it has to be explained, it can't be."

M. R. MONTGOMERY

A fly fisher shrugs, unable to explain the inscrutable allure of his sport.

"I honestly don't know why I fish. Or, rather, I fish in order to save my life; I just don't know <u>why</u> it saves my life."

John Gierach

Another fly fishing life is saved along California's Hat Creek.

R. Valentine Atkinson

11

> "Many go fishing all their lives without knowing it is not fish they are after."
>
> HENRY DAVID THOREAU

A fly-hooked trout makes a run in this Currier & Ives lithograph.

The American Magazine
APRIL ★ 25 CENTS
Thirty Cents in Canada

AGATHA CHRISTIE

JOHN BARRYMORE

JOHN ERSKINE

IRVIN COBB

KATHLEEN NORRIS

"The point of all other fishing was to bring home meat, but with a fly line the process is itself the purpose. The elegance of casting justified the endeavor, regardless of the catch."

WAYNE FIELDS

American illustrator Penrhyn Stanlaws (1877–1957) created this graceful image for the April 1933 issue of The American Magazine.

"Some wiseguy once defined a fishing line as a piece of string with a worm on one end and a damn fool on the other. This is a silly definition, of course—for many fishermen use flies instead of worms."

ED ZERN

A fishing line is tested—and holds true—on this vintage Victorian trade card for Merrick Thread Company.

He can't break it George, it's Merrick's Best Six Cord Thread. Best in the World.

"Theodore Gordon introduced the dry fly to this country with a batch of imitation insects he got from England in 1890. Before then trout were caught the way you'd expect, with a w——m on a hook, or wet flies, and neither fish nor fishermen got neurotic about it."

GEORGE TICHENOR

Blissfully unaware of wet or dry flies, a carefree boy carries home his bounty in this lithograph by James C. McKell (1885–1956).

15

> "I fish not because
> I regard fishing as
> being terribly impor-
> tant, but because I
> suspect that so many
> of the other concerns
> of men are equally
> unimportant, and not
> nearly so much fun."

JOHN VOELKER
WRITING AS
ROBERT TRAVER

*A trio of fly fishermen gear
up for a day on the river.*

R. Valentine Atkinson

16

Bob White

"Fly-fishing is the most fun you can have standing up."

ARNOLD GINGRICH

Fly fishers play a pair of Alaskan king salmon on a small river that drains into the Bering Sea.

17

> "Our tradition is that of the first man who sneaked away to the creek when the tribe did not really need fish."
>
> RODERICK HAIG-BROWN

R. Valentine Atkinson

Fly rod in hand, a modern-day angler sneaks away for a day's fishing.

"Fishing is much more than fish. . . . It is the great occasion when we may return to the fine simplicity of our forefathers."

HERBERT HOOVER

A fly fisherman poses with his quarry in this wood engraving dating from the late 1800s.

> "Rivers and the inhabitants of the watery elements are made for wise men to contemplate and for fools to pass by without consideration."
>
> Izaak Walton

The grandfather of fly fishing, Sir Izaak Walton penned The Compleat Angler *in 1653. This wood engraving, created by Louis Rhead circa 1900, depicts the great angler teaching the gentle sport to a scholar.*

Courtesy of the Library of Congress

"One may drive to the camp in an old car or a jeep but, after that, elementary democracy sets in; all fishermen alike must walk down to the big river—even the arrogant new jeepocracy."

JOHN VOELKER WRITING AS ROBERT TRAVER

R. Valentine Atkinson

A party of anglers hikes in for a day of fly fishing.

> "Calling fly fishing a hobby is like calling brain surgery a job."
>
> PAUL SCHULLERY

Magnifier clipped to his hat brim, a fly fisherman performs the delicate procedure of tying on a fly before casting into California's Burney Creek.

"The fish is the boss you thought you left behind. It will dispense with your fly like a good suggestion."

JARED SANDBERG

This 1950s-era ink blotter features an angler tying on a winning fly.

"The river has always been a metaphor for life. In its movement, in its varied glides, runs, and pools, in its inevitable progress toward the sea, it contains many of the secrets we seek to understand about ourselves, our purposes."

NICK LYONS

An angler studies the Upper Sacramento River in California, renowned for its fly fishing.

R. Valentine Atkinson

24

APRIL, 1907

PRICE 15 CENTS

FIELD AND STREAM

COVER DESIGN BY PAUL BRANSOM

"A fish, which you can't see, deep down in the water, is a kind of symbol of peace on earth, good will to yourself."

ROBERT RUARK

Known as the "Dean of America's Wildlife Artists," Paul Bransom (1885–1979) provided cover art for myriad books and magazines during America's golden age of illustration.

"Fly-fishing for wild trout on quiet waters must be one of the toughest and craziest ways to catch fish ever invented by man, as well as among the most frustrating and humiliating."

JOHN VOELKER
WRITING AS
ROBERT TRAVER

Wildlife artist Churchill Ettinger (1903–1984) captures one of trout-fishing's more humiliating moments.

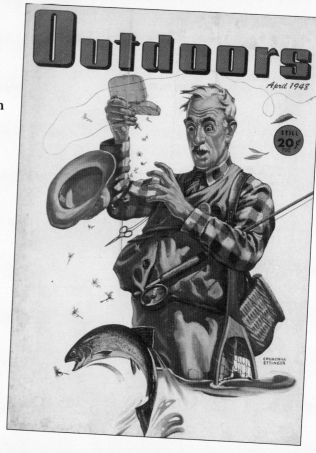

> "What's that Walton said about fishing being a 'contemplative man's quiet recreation?' It's the most bloody frustrating thing I've ever done."
>
> JAMES PROSEK

This commissioned watercolor painting is wryly titled First Cast of the Day.

"In all my years of fly fishing I've never encountered an expert, have come to believe they don't exist."

W. D. WETHERELL

No experts, these fishing pals simply enjoy their "daytime, playtime hours" in this 1950 Hanes ad.

Sports Ho!

Here are the New SUEDEKNITS for those extra sports hours this summer

Treat yourself to color and comfort for those daytime, playtime hours after work and on week-ends. Slip into a Hanes SUEDEKNIT. Styled by a top men's fashion designer. Knit for action-in-sports by Hanes—makers, for 19 years, of fine underwear for men and boys.

SUEDEKNIT is as soft as suede. It has the "feel" of fine Cashmere. Superb workmanship reflects the fine values you expect from Hanes. All colors fast to sun and tub. You just can't buy better knit sportswear. So *why* pay *more* than Hanes bake-to-buyer prices?

*Reg. U. S. Pat. Off.

A. SUEDEKNIT CREW NECK TWO TONE SHIRT. Gray body. Collarette and sleeve trim: Navy Blue, Burgundy or Green, $1.75

B. SUEDEKNIT OPEN COLLAR SHIRT. Body of Sierra Blue, Birch Gray, Canary or White, with harmonizing striped tab insert. $2.50

C. SUEDEKNIT GAUCHO COLLAR SHIRT. Vent front with looped button. Choose from Palomino Tan, Sierra Blue, Champagne, Birch Gray, Canary, White, Fairway Green and Marlin Blue. $2.25. SUEDEKNIT CREW NECK SHIRT. Same colors. $1.50, Rocky Mt. & West, $1.50

D. SUEDEKNIT TWO TONE "V" SHIRT. Choice of Champagne, Canary, Birch Gray and Sierra Blue, each with harmonizing "V" panel. $1.95, Rocky Mt. & West, $2.00

WORTH SHOPPING FOR! AT GOOD STORES THROUGHOUT AMERICA   Sportswear • Underwear for men and boys • Children's sleepers • P. H. Hanes Knitting Co., Winston-Salem 1, N. C.

"There's no taking trout with dry breeches."

Miguel de Cervantes, *Don Quixote*

A trout fisherman gets a dousing in this vintage painting signed Hy Hintermeister. Famed for their humorous outdoors-themed art, father-and-son team John Henry Hintermeister (1870–1945) and Henry Adamaugust Hintermeister (1897–1972) created many paintings under this pseudonym.

"Never believe a fisherman when he tells you that he does not care about the fish he catches. ... And why not? ... When you have good luck in anything, you ought to be glad. Indeed, if you are not glad, you are not really lucky."

HENRY VAN DYKE

A lucky fisherman poses with his fly-caught rainbow trout before releasing it back into southwestern Alaska's Grant River.

Bob White

Schlitz *with food and fun and sun!*
Outsells them all

Schlitz

What a wonderful way to put thirst in the shade, Schlitz!

World over, more people choose this superb refresher than any other beer, at any price.

Schlitz is the smart way to cool off. It fills thirst, but never you.

Even with the heartiest meal you can enjoy a glass of Schlitz. There's no filling. Schlitz is brewed that way. Brisk, stand-up flavor, smoothed by just the kiss of the hops. All beer, and yet light. So light. No bitterness.

You, too! Keep Schlitz cooling at home.

THE BEER THAT MADE MILWAUKEE FAMOUS

© 1956 Jos. Schlitz Brewing Co., Milwaukee, Wis., Brooklyn, N. Y., Los Angeles, California

"My wife wonders why all women do not seek anglers for husbands. She has come in contact with many in her life with me and she claims that they all have a sweetness in their nature which others lack."

RAY BERGMAN

A happy couple take a break from the river in this 1956 Schlitz ad.

> "Give a man a trout and you can feed him for a day. Teach him how to fly fish and you can sell him gear for a lifetime."
>
> PROVERB

Fly rod and reel, boots, hat, fishing vest, fly box—these are only a few of the items needed to embark upon the great sport of fly fishing.

R. Valentine Atkinson

"The great charm of fly-fishing is that we are always learning."

Theodore Gordon

Fly fishing is one of the many skills students can learn at Penn State. Here, legendary angling professor Joe Humphreys demonstrates, in Angling 109, some of the finer points of casting.

"You may practice catch-and-release as a religion, but that doesn't mean the next person has to bow down to your god."

PETER KAMINSKY

The warden has the final word in this vintage print by American illustrator Joseph Kernan (1878–1958).

"If you have never picked up a fly rod before, you will soon find it factually and theologically true that man by nature is a damn mess."

NORMAN MACLEAN

Trout on the line, a novice angler seeks belated counsel in this vintage Hy Hintermeister print.

"A perfect day is often measured in minutes and sometimes only seconds. A good example is that rare cast to a rising fish ordinarily beyond our modest reach, when the timing of the double haul and the lift of a sweet breeze sends the fly out to a rarified distance, with the loops as tight as a clothespin, the fly tugging at the backing knot and then drifting down on the water as softly as a wish."

GENE HILL

Fly line floating overhead, an angler on Yellowstone River experiences a perfect moment.

Bob White

"And there is nothing quite like the feeling that comes over you when a fish takes a fly you have tied: disbelief, then delight, and finally smug satisfaction!"

JOAN WULFF

Posing on a remote Alaska stream, a proud angler displays her quarry.

> "Trout fishing for me is not the taking of fish, but being at one with the stream and all the sights and sounds."
>
> SIGURD OLSON

Eldridge Hardie

Early Risers, *a watercolor by sporting artist Eldridge Hardie, evokes the peaceful beauty of a solitary morning's fly fishing.*

"More than half the intense enjoyment of fly-fishing is derived from the beautiful surroundings, the satisfaction felt from being in the open air, the new lease of life secured thereby."

CHARLES F. ORVIS

Charles Orvis grew up fishing Vermont's famed Battenkill River. In 1856, he founded the company that leads the nation in outfitting fly fishers with high-end clothing and gear.

R. Valentine Atkinson

39

> "Never, either with a rod or with a gun, have I found a tougher challenge than the precise shot of the fly to a cruising bonefish."
>
> CHARLES ELLIOTT

A saltwater angler pursues bonefish in the flats surrounding Christmas Island.

R. Valentine Atkinson

"Limiting your fly fishing to trout is like limiting your beer drinking to lager."

TERRY HACKETT

In celebration of mayfly season, a Guinness is served adorned with the delicate, short-lived insect.

> **"All Americans believe that they are born fishermen. For a man to admit to a distaste for fishing would be like denouncing mother-love and hating moonlight."**
>
> JOHN STEINBECK

Bob White

In addition to penning such great American classics as The Grapes of Wrath *(1939), Steinbeck was an avid fly fisherman. Here, artist Bob White captures an angler making that final cast by the light of the moon.*

"To me heaven would be a big bull ring with me holding two barrera seats and a trout stream outside that no one else was allowed to fish in."

ERNEST HEMINGWAY

Steam rises around a morning angler fly fishing at Nez Perce Ford in the Yellowstone River. Hemingway's literary antiheroes famously sought such trout-rich waters.

"The dry fly man has passed through all of the stages of the angler's life, from the cane pole and the drop-line to the split bamboo and the fur-and feather counterfeit of the midge fly."

George LaBranche

Farmer. "THERE'S A BIG UN OVER YONDER. WHY DON'T YE 'AVE A GOO AT 'E?"
Dry Fly Purist. "AH! FARIO TAKING NYMPHÆ. NO GOOD AT ALL."
Farmer. "ONE O' THEM EDICATED FISH, I PRESOOM?"

Cartoonist Frank Reynolds (1876–1953) created this cartoon in 1921 for the venerable British humor magazine Punch, or the London Charivari.

"It's not a purist thing at all. It's just that the sight of a good fish inhaling your cocky floating fly raises hackles in a way a twitch of the fluffy floating indicator cannot."

James R. Babb

R. Valentine Atkinson

Many consider trout fishing with dry flies, such as those pictured here, to be the highest form of piscatorial pursuit.

"Often, I have been exhausted on trout streams, uncomfortable, wet, cold, briar scarred, sunburned, mosquito-bitten, but never, with a fly rod in my hand, have I been in a place that was less than beautiful."

CHARLES KURALT

A fly fisherman treads rushing waters amidst breathtaking surroundings.

R. Valentine Atkinson

"Land a good trout or bass, hold it for a second on the wet skin of your hand, and you have, in one compact bundle, as beautiful and bewildering a combination of opposites as it's possible to imagine; strength and litheness, fragility and toughness, intelligence and obtuseness, fastidiousness and voraciousness, boldness and stealth."

W. D. Wetherall

Bob White

Bob White's original painting captures a moment of connection between brown trout and angler.

"All the romance of trout fishing exists in the mind of the angler and is in no way shared by the fish."

<small>HAROLD F. BLAISDELL</small>

A debonair angler poses with his catch in this historical photograph.

49

"Fly patterns are a lot like women. Some are plain. Some are flashy and some are in between."

JIMMY D. MOORE

Legendary American pin-up artist Gil Elvgren (1914–1980) created this glamorous image for the Louis F. Dow calendar company in 1937.

"Chasing trout is no less wearing and barely less complicated than chasing women."

JOHN VOELKER
WRITING AS
ROBERT TRAVER

A Double Catch is a Vaughan Bass pin-up created circa 1950 for Louis F. Dow & Co.

51

"**If fishing is a religion, fly fishing is high church.**"

TOM BROKAW

The glorious sunbathed cliffs surrounding Washington's Lake Lenore double as a house of worship for early morning fly fishers.

Dennis Frates

> "Fishing is my religion and the trout stream is my temple."
>
> JAMES PROSEK

Rainbow trout glide underwater in an Oregon waterway.

Dennis Frates

> "Somebody just back of you while you are fishing is as bad as someone looking over your shoulder while you write a letter to your girl."
>
> ERNEST HEMINGWAY

An angler attempts to ignore his spectators in Fisherman's Luck, *a vintage Hy Hintermeister print.*

> **"Testing oneself is best when done alone."**
>
> Jimmy Carter, "Trout"

A devoted trout fisherman, President Carter enjoyed the challenge of fishing with a fly. Here, an angler confronts one of those angling moments best experienced by oneself.

"You are to know that there are so many sorts of flies as there be of fruits . . . indeed too many either for me to name, or for you to remember: and their breeding is so various and wonderful, that I might easily amaze myself, and tire you in a relation of them."

Izaak Walton

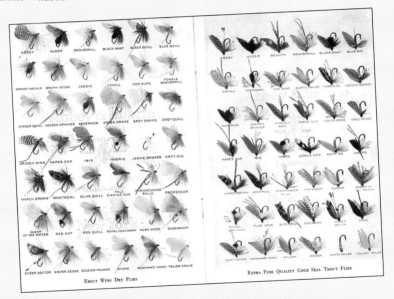

This 1929 advertisement by Abbey & Imbrie, the esteemed tackle company, features a dazzling array of eighty-four different flies.

"I'm never convinced I've got the right fly—unless there's a fish attached—which is seldom."

GENE HILL

Two anglers consider the merits of a selected fly.

R. Valentine Atkinson

> "Anglers ... exaggerate grossly and make gentle and inoffensive creatures sound like wounded buffalo and man-eating tigers."

RODERICK HAIG-BROWN

A fly fisherman battles a fearsome trout in this 1965 Schmidt's advertisement.

"All fishermen are liars; it's an occupational disease with them like housemaid's knee or editor's ulcers."

BEATRICE COOK

A fly fisherman secures a prize trout to his vehicle in this vintage postcard created at Fields Photo Shop.

> "The modern fly rod ... is a piece of magic, an elegant thing, willowy and alive—a wand that when held in the hand communicates with the heart."
>
> HOWELL RAINES

This 1931 Montague advertisement shows off the graceful arc of a Redwing fly rod.

"Even now, after nearly forty years, I will still occasionally refer to a three-hundred-dollar custom-built fly rod as a fish pole."

PATRICK McMANUS

R. Valentine Atkinson

Beautiful fly rods adorn the wall of a fishing camp.

"In 1918 I realized that the growing use of the automobile, with its easy transportation, would soon spoil all public trout fishing."

EDWARD R. HEWITT

Automobiles bring anglers right to the river's edge in these ads for the 1917 Chandler Six and the 1952 Chevrolet Styleline.

62

Here's one that will change your ideas about how much a fine car need cost

Let's forget the price angle—just for a moment!—and see how this 1952 Chevrolet measures up as a car you'd be proud to own and drive.

Rate it on appearance, with an eye to the fine details of construction that make Chevrolet's Body by Fisher the quality standard of the low-price field. Notice, too, that color has been brought inside the car to provide brighter, more attractive interiors.

Take it out on the road, and discover for yourself the exciting new sensation of smoothness. Engine vibration has been "screened out"

(Continuation of standard equipment and trim illustrated is dependent on availability of material)

to bring you the thrill of new Centerpoise Power. New Quick-Reflex shock absorber action gives a smoother, softer ride.

Test the brakes—largest in Chevrolet's field. See how easily this car handles—steering control is *centered* between the front wheels. And enjoy Powerglide automatic transmission—wonderfully simple, simply wonderful!

Here is pleasure unlimited . . . *in the lowest-priced line in the low-price field.* No wonder more people buy Chevrolets than any other car! See your Chevrolet dealer and save. Chevrolet Division of General Motors, Detroit 2, Michigan.

Landing a beauty—it's a Spring Green Styleline De Luxe 4-Door Sedan. Harmonizing two-tone green interior . . . smart, attractive, inviting.

Out for "Muskies." After a tussle with these fresh-water fighters, you'll be thankful for the restful comfort of Chevrolet's softer Knee-Action ride.

Surf casting. Thrilling as your first drive with Powerglide. Teamed with extra-powerful Valve-in-Head engine, new Automatic Choke. Optional on De Luxe models, extra cost.

The Only Fine Cars **PRICED SO LOW!**

SEE THE DINAH SHORE SHOW ON TELEVISION
Every Tuesday and Thursday Evenings, NBC-TV Network.

Weighing in a Blue Marlin. Plenty of people who can afford the most costly cars prefer to drive a Chevrolet. It's thoroughly satisfying!

> "People are easy to fool. The real test comes when you try the fly out on a fish."
>
> LOUISE DICKINSON RICH

Fishing partners swap tall tales in this 1956 Corby's Whiskey ad.

Easy tie-in that nets pleasure

THERE'S NO surer way of hauling in the big ones than tying up a batch of your own flies, Mr. Fisherman. And to make any session with the hooks and feathers a big success, call in your fishing cronies—and serve up sociable Corby's whiskey. Corby's fine flavor is enjoyed by fishermen and millions of other sportsmen. Next time, assure yourself of a net return in pleasure—say "Corby's."

Time to say CORBY'S

Look for the parrot on every bottle of Corby's, one of America's favorite whiskeys.

BLENDED WHISKEY—86 PROOF—68.4% GRAIN NEUTRAL SPIRITS—JAS. BARCLAY & CO. LIMITED, PEORIA, ILL.

"If there is anything genuinely humorous about fishing, it is that of a serious angler selecting a fly to exchange for the one he is discarding."

BURTON SPILLER

A fly fisherman attempts to match the hatch on California's Hat Creek.

R. Valentine Atkinson

"Handling a big trout in swift water is akin to flying a kite on a blustery day. The more line you let out, the more trouble you're going to have getting it back."

Jimmy D. Moore

A novice fly fisher makes the best of a tangled situation on the Grant River at the headwaters of the Wood River drainage.

Bob White

"Listen to the sound of the river and you will get a trout."

IRISH PROVERB

Colorado's White River rushes around two anglers pausing to select new flies.

R. Valentine Atkinson

67

"The strike is electrifying, yes, but the leap gives a fisherman wings."

JERRY GIBBS

A brown trout leaps in an effort to shake itself free of an Alder wet fly.

Doug Stamm

> "The climax in the poem of trouting is the spring of the split bamboo."
>
> LEWIS B. FRANCE

A fly rod flexes in this Victorian trade card from the 1800s.

69

"One who has learned to cast the fly seldom if ever returns to the days when he was content to sit upon the bank, or the string-piece of a pier, dangling his legs overboard while he watched his cork bobbing up and down, indicating by its motions what might be happening to the bunch of worms at the hook end of the line."

GEORGE LABRANCHE

A fisherman immerses himself in the angling experience on this vintage ink blotter.

A GALLANT FIGHTER

MAC'S *Thrifty* STORE

James McLaren

WORK CLOTHING — SPORT WEAR

"YOUR MONEY'S WORTH
OR YOUR MONEY BACK"

78 N. COURT ST.   ATHENS, OHIO

Across from Nye Chevrolet Used Car Lot

"O, sir, doubt not that Angling is an art; is it not an art to deceive a trout with an artificial fly?"

IZAAK WALTON

Artful peacock feathers are used to tie artificial flies, along with feathers from chickens, ducks, grouse, ostriches, partridges, pheasants, turkeys, and more.

Dennis Frates

71

> "There is certainly something in angling that tends to produce a serenity of the mind."
>
> WASHINGTON IRVING

The July 1915 cover of Pictorial Review *magazine features a contented angler gazing upon a red ibis fly.*

PICTORIAL REVIEW

A NEW SERIAL
BY
ELEANOR
HALLOWELL
ABBOTT
IN THIS ISSUE

JULY 1915
FIFTEEN CENTS

THE PICTORIAL REVIEW COMPANY, NEW YORK

Courtesy of George Fraley

"Oh, the gallant fisher's life!
It is the best of any;
'T is full of pleasure, void of strife,
And 't is beloved by many."

JOHN CHALKHILL

This idealistic image, Fly-fishing for Trout, *was created by British artist James Pollard (1792–1867) and "Dedicated to the Members of the Waltonian Society, by a Brother Angler."*

"There is something about rain. Especially a warm rain, spilled over a city or a network of trout streams. It kindles a spark. It presses a button. It is an urgent message from afar to any seeker of the holy grail of anglingdom— trout."

GORDON MACQUARRIE

A fly fisher responds to the call of rain in this sketch advertising the Sou'wester, a hat designed to angle rainwater away from the body.

"The two best times to fish is when it's rainin' and when it ain't."

Patrick McManus

Bob White

A fly fisher holds his ground in this evocative painting, Rain.

"The art of fly casting always makes me think of dancing and therefore it seems more feminine than masculine."

Joan Wulff

Chesterfield uses fly fishing in this 1939 cigarette advertisement to evoke graceful femininity.

THE SATURDAY EVENING POST

Chesterfield

...the catch of the season
for more smoking pleasure

In every part of the country smokers are turning to Chesterfields for what they really want in a cigarette...*refreshing mildness...better taste...and a more pleasing aroma.*

"It was painful business, learning to cast without hanging the flies in the trees, conquering the clumsiness of foot that is as much an enemy in wading as in dancing."

HOWELL RAINES

Fly line coils around the feet of an angler preparing to shoot lots of line.

"It is not a fish until it is on the bank."

<small>IRISH PROVERB</small>

Cutthroat trout line the bank in this photo postcard by Pacific Northwest photographer Ross Hall (1905–1990).

"Among freshwater game fish, the bass is the neighborhood tough who wears a derby hat, smokes big, black cigars and never shaves."

RED SMITH

A largemouth bass emerges from the depths in pursuit of a Porky's Pet bass bug.

Doug Stamm

79

"Ours is the grandest sport. It is an intriguing battle of wits between an angler and a trout."

ERNEST G. SCHWIEBERT JR.

A fly fisher battles a worthy opponent in this vintage tackle ad.

"To paraphrase a deceased patriot, I regret that I have but one life to give to my fly-fishing."

JOHN VOELKER
WRITING AS
ROBERT TRAVER

A World War II soldier displays his catch of Dolly Varden and salmon in this 1943 photograph.

"Some things in life can't really be explained. Like a belief in God or what love is or, maybe, how you catch a trout with a nymph."

WILLIAM PLUMMER

Club members talk religion, love, and fly fishing at the picturesque River Otter Club in California.

R. Valentine Atkinson

"I found myself thinking back over the years and thanking the heavens I'd come to be where I was, knee-deep in a trout stream with a fly rod in my hand."

BILL BARICH

Richard Vander Meer

An angler strips in line in this original painting by Canadian artist Richard Vander Meer.

"**Any fly fisher knows that you can't always count on the fish to cooperate, but you can always count on a good beer when the day is done.**"

TERRY HACKETT

A celebratory beer tops off a day's fly fishing in this 1953 Miller High Life advertisement.

"Well, here's to better luck tomorrow!"

DRY *Paul Jones*...a gentleman's whiskey since 1865

IN a whiskey as in a champagne or a sherry, dryness has just one purpose. To bring out true flavor. Paul Jones's dryness (lack of sweetness) brings out all the richness and mellowness of this very fine American whiskey.

A blend of straight whiskies—90 proof. Frankfort Distillers Corporation, New York City.

"Like good whisky
most fly fishing
stories are a blend
of the old and
the new."

CAPTAIN PAUL DARBY

*Fly fishing gear in
a 1944 Paul Jones
advertisement evokes
a day on the river.*

85

"Fooling around with an old fishing vest is rather like robbing a grave. You are violating sacred ground."

Gene Hill

Bob White

This original watercolor, Alaskan Memories, *pays homage to a far-flung fishing trip.*

*S*moothest way to "rough it"

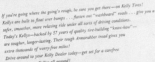

KELLY *Springfield* **TIRES**

*If you're going where the going's rough, be sure you get there—on Kelly Tires!
Kellys are built to float over bumps . . . flatten out "washboard" roads . . . give you a
safer, smoother, more relaxing ride under all sorts of driving conditions.
Today's Kellys—backed by 57 years of quality tire-building "know-how"—
are tougher, longer-lasting. Their tough Armorubber tread gives you
extra thousands of worry-free miles!
Drive around to your Kelly Dealer today—get set for a carefree
summer with new Kellys all around!*

Proved and improved for 57 years

THE KELLY-SPRINGFIELD TIRE COMPANY, CUMBERLAND 3, MARYLAND

"The most indispensable item in any fisherman's equipment is his hat."

COREY FORD

Colorful flies adorn an angler's hat in this 1951 Kelly Tires ad.

87

> "Game fish are too valuable to be caught only once."
>
> LEE WULFF

A founding father of today's catch-and-release programs, conservationist Lee Wulff helped spark, in the 1930s, a new attitude toward game fish. Here, anglers release a fly-caught cutthroat back into the Snake River.

R. Valentine Atkinson

Dennis Frates

"If something wonderful isn't about to happen, then why the hell are we all standing around like this?"

JOHN GIERACH

A mass of fly fishers crowd Washington's Lake Lenore.

> "Fish are, of course, indispensable to the angler. They give him an excuse for fishing and justify the flyrod without which he would be a mere vagrant."

ALFRED MILLER
WRITING AS
SPARSE GREY HACKLE

A fisherman poses in 1929 with a steelhead caught in California's Klamath River.

> "When a man picks up a fly rod for the first time, he may not know it but he has been born again."

JOSEPH D. FARRIS

R. Valentine Atkinson

An angler clutches a handful of beautifully crafted Orvis fly rods.

> "There is something deep in the human spirit that responds to running water. The trout fisherman knows it well."
>
> A. J. McCLANE

R. Valentine Atkinson

The rushing waters of Mossbrae Falls beckon fly fishers the world over to California's Upper Sacramento River.

R. Valentine Atkinson

"A stream is music and motion: smooth glides, fast, turbulent riffles and deep pools, each posing a special challenge."

NELSON BRYANT

A trout stream winds through a bucolic landscape.

93

"There are fishing tournaments, contest and pools, to be sure, but ... by far the most rewarding forms of competition in angling are those that take place between the fish and the angler, and within the angler himself."

JAMES WESTMAN

Sporting artist Tom Rost (1909–2004) conveys the mayhem of a fly fishing tournament in his April 1952 Field & Stream *cover painting.*

> "No misanthropist, I must nevertheless confess that I like and frequently prefer to fish alone."

JOHN VOELKER WRITING AS ROBERT TRAVER

R. Valentine Atkinson

A lone angler stalks the sere shores of Hat Creek.

"There is no greater fan of fly fishing than the worm."

Patrick McManus

Another worm is spared as an angler consults his fly box over Burney Creek.

R. Valentine Atkinson

96

BEY　　ALDER　　BEAVERKILL　　BLACK GNAT　　BLACK QUILL　　BLUE QUILL

HACKLE　　BROWN SEDGE　　CADDIS　　CAHILL　　COW DUNG　　FEMALE BEAVERKILL

QUILL　　GOLDEN SPINNER　　GOVERNOR　　GREEN DRAKE　　GREY DRAKE　　GREY QUILL

KING　　HARE'S EAR　　IBIS　　IMBRIE　　JENNIE SPINNER　　KATY DID

TRADE MARK

Established 1820